NORMANDO HERNÁNDEZ GONZÁLEZ:

7 YEARS IN PRISON FOR WRITING ABOUT BREAD

Adam Braver and Molly Gessford
Translated by Cynthia Guardado

Printed in the United States of America

Adam Braver and Molly Gessford
Translated by Cynthia Guardado

Normando Hernández González:
7 Years in Prison for Writing About Bread

ISBN: 978-1-60801-087-5

Book Design by Allison Reu
Cover Design by Alex Dimeff

Photos © 2012:
Alana Conn: Pages 12, 101, 103, 147, 176, 177.
Courtesy of Normando Hernández González: Pages 32, 34, 115, 161, 172, 175.

Cover Photo © Corbis.

UNO PRESS

unopress.org

University of New Orleans Press

Portions of this book have appeared in the *Normal School.*

Foreword

On March 18, 2003, as the world was bracing for the United States' invasion of Iraq, Fidel Castro launched a crackdown on critical voices in his own country that came to be known as the Black Spring. Within days, seventy-five of Cuba's most important dissidents, including twenty-nine journalists, were behind bars; within a month, they had all been handed sentences from six to twenty-eight years in prison. It was one of the most brazen, wholesale violations of the universally-guaranteed right to freedom of expression in recent memory, and one of the most opportunistic and cynical rights violations I have ever seen.

The youngest of the seventy-five, Normando Hernández González was thirty-two years old when he was tried with three others in a one-day proceeding on May 4, 2003 and sentenced to twenty-five years in prison. His crimes, as enumerated in the sentencing document, included contributing reports on the "economic-political-social order" of the Cuban state to Radio José Martí, the website CUBANET, and such other "counterrevolutionary" media outlets as the *Miami Herald*, Agence France-Presse, Reuters, and CNN, and receiving a fax machine and medicines from James Cason, the head of the U.S. Interests Section in Havana—the latter of which he allegedly distributed "with the intention of winning addicts to his cause." Like all who dedicate themselves to providing independent reportage in Cuba—Normando not only dispatched his own stories but also directed the College of Independent

Journalists of Camagüey—he knew the reward for his efforts was almost certainly prison; when the crackdown began, he eluded arrest just long enough to celebrate his daughter's first birthday and then turned himself in.

Seven years later, Normando and the fifty-one other Black Spring casualties still in prison were released and sent to Spain under a deal brokered by the Spanish government and the Catholic Church. That deal was driven by political and economic calculations on both sides of the Atlantic. But driving those calculations—making them calculations at all—was a human force that is embodied by this book's authors.

For more than a year, Adam Braver, who writes novels and teaches creative writing at Roger Williams University, and Molly Gessford and ten of her fellow writing students (along with photographer and teacher Jeffrey Silverthorne) had been pressing Normando's case. On their own, in just one year, they managed to make their voices heard in Washington, in Havana, and in the prison cells and hospital rooms between which Normando was shuffled that year as his physical condition deteriorated. What they said, and what thousands like them around the world said over the course of those seven years, was simple: Normando Hernández González and his colleagues are unjustly imprisoned and must be set free.

And because Castro jailed Normando to silence him, when Normando was released at last, Adam and Molly did something more: they traveled to Spain to hear him speak. It is that basic and profoundly restorative gesture that gives rise to this remarkable book, the most fitting tribute I can imagine to Normando's idealism, grace, and incredible courage and to our common humanity.

—Larry Siems
Author of *The Torture Report*
Former Director of PEN American Center's
Freedom to Write &
International Programs
New York, NY

Introduction

"My name is Normando Hernández González. I am 41 years of age. I am an independent Cuban journalist. And a former prisoner of conscience." Thus began three days of conversations in late March 2011, chronicling the past decade of Normando's life, the majority of it spent incarcerated in Cuban prisons for his writing.

* * *

We were a little nervous when the translator told us we were part of it now. It was in Normando's apartment in Madrid, and we really didn't know where we were, only that we'd gotten off the Metro at the Villa de Vallecas stop, and come up the escalator, and then had been told to wait on the Federico Lorca plaza once we'd phoned to say we'd made it that far. We'd waited for what seemed like a long time. Then came another phone call, telling us it would be a few more minutes. To kill time, we strolled to a shoe store across the plaza, lingering, holding up boots on the outside sale rack, trying to mentally convert the sizes, too embarrassed to try to speak Spanish with the clerks who were running mops around us, as they prepared to open the store. We went back to the mouth of the subway to wait it out. It was morning. Already it was hot. The same skinny African man had walked by us at least three times, then took a seat on a bench to our right, not quite relaxed, his knee bouncing up and down. He kept a watch on us the whole time.

Finally, Normando, Normando's uncle, and the translator, met us. Together, we walked to a park, where Normando's wife, Yaraí, along with other exiled Ladies in White[1], gathered for an international day of honor for their work. Journalists interviewed Normando, Yaraí, and the other women. His nine year-old daughter Daniela ran around the park, playing with the children.

After about a half-hour, we followed Normando to his apartment, walking down streets bordered by vacant lots, one where a boy played, jailed by a collapsed wire fence, trying to bat a rock with a stick. Older subsidized-looking apartment buildings popped up here and there, with worn orange siding. Compared to central Madrid, it felt desolate and a little more hopeless. And it was quiet. Each sound held its own place. Hardly talking, we passed another dried grass field where a sloppy girl who might have been pretty stood with one hand on her hip, and the other pressing a phone to her ear while her two dogs relieved themselves in dusty weed patches. She smiled at us and shrugged her shoulders. We turned a corner onto a street filled with tenements and went up into the building through a door that would look completely different when we'd finally come out six hours later.

1 In 2005, the European Union awarded the Sakharov Prize for Freedom of Thought to the Ladies in White, noting that since the 2004 formation of *Las Damas de blanco*, the wives and daughters of the Black Spring journalists have "brought international attention to the issue by their peaceful protests every Sunday."

* * *

For the previous year, we had been working as case minders with the PEN American Center on Normando's case, following the counsel of Larry Siems, director of PEN's Freedom to Write and International programs, and his staff, Anna Kushner and Sarah Hoffman. It was a part of a "living class" at Roger Williams University, colloquially known as the PEN Collaborative. As case minders, the group participated in monitoring Normando's case, letter writing campaigns to Cuban officials and others of influence, and face-to-face with visits with officials from the State Department, the White House, and members of Congress[2]. During that time, he had still been in prison, and his health was deteriorating; his survival was in question. After starting a successful Facebook presence, we connected with his mother, Blanca, who was living in Florida. Between her and PEN, we were able to continue to work on his case with the stamina and belief that he might actually be freed—although quietly, we weren't certain that he would survive. At that year's commencement, the university awarded Normando its President's Core Values Medallion. Later that week in New York, Cuba's Permanent Mission to the United Nations not only refused to forward the award to Normando in prison but also refused us entry into their offices. Despite some positive momentum, things were not looking good; particularly given the ticking time bomb of Normando's health, which seemed to be further in decline, resulting in the removal of his gallbladder, after being afflicted with pedunculated polyps, and severe weight loss. But then, moving into early summer, there were hints that a release might be negotiated. Everybody was cautious. This kind of chatter was not unusual but often fruitless. Yet on July 6, 2010, an email arrived from Anna Kushner at PEN: *Normando is freed!!!!* Following his release, Normando began exchanging emails with us. From there began the idea of meeting, as well as having a formal conversation.

---

2 It should be noted that U.S. Senators Sheldon Whitehouse (D-RI) and Jack Reed (D-RI) co-authored a letter to Raúl Castro, advocating for Normando's release on humanitarian grounds.

* * *

On that first day, we were both tired from a flight the day before that had taken three times as long as it should have to get there. We'd barely slept, and the day was six hours ahead of what we were used to. But our complaints were minor in the larger picture. Despite barely having money, Normando and Yaraí had opened their home to us. They set up the table with platters of potato chips, ham slices, and nuts. There was beer and soda, as well. Out the window, we could see the señora across the street on the balcony, hanging brightly colored laundry over the railing. She peered in at us on occasion, a little curious, but she didn't seem to care.

Then Normando began his story, focused particularly on his first year in prison. It was lousy with beatings. Lousy with psychological torture. And lousy with the truth of how easily people will give up their decency in order to strip someone else of his dignity.

* * *

We talked for hours on end in his cramped apartment in this working class Vallecas district of Madrid, a functional flat provided by the Spanish government and furnished by charitable donations, giving it a sense of transience. He'd only been out of jail for about six months, and, for all intents and purposes, he was exiled in Spain. It was a very in-between time, filled with contradictions. While he was reunited with his wife and daughter, he was a stranger in a foreign country, separated from his mother in the United States. While he was free to walk the streets as he pleased, he was living in poverty, relying on temporary funds from the Spanish government, a subsidy that always seemed to be in flux. And while his goal simply was to get to the U.S., he was caught in endless circular mazes of bureaucracy, leaving him to feel like a different kind of prisoner. Everything was still very raw. It was too soon for reflection. Even when smiling or breaking into infectious laughter, his eyes remain steeled.

* * *

When the translator said the thing about being *part of it now*, the tape recorder was off. He said, "I'm just warning you." He took a handful of chips. "These are serious circumstances."

We talked until the translator said he'd run out of steam. He was much older than the rest of us. He had diabetes, and he needed to rest. Although we said nothing, we also were worn out. The lack of sleep coupled with the intensity of the interview and the heat of the day had finally gotten to us.

* * *

Apparently the translator had been very helpful since Normando and his family had arrived in Spain. He'd set up them up in this apartment, arranged for clothing donations, and represented him when there were issues with the government. He seemed to know people.

We planned for Normando to meet up with us at our apartment in Chamberí the next day. The translator told us it would be nice if we could cover Normando's Metro ride. Then he showed us a monthly statement from the Spanish government that was on Normando's desk. It looked heavily bureaucratic with its logos and line items, yet it looked strangely individualized, not like a form letter off the computer. It was on thin onionskin typing paper, and though the lettering likely came from a word processor, it seemed to have an imperfect human touch; plus the page was wrinkled, as though a dozen hands had touched it. Judging by the initials at the bottom, at least four different ones had.

The upshot was a complex political relationship between Spain and Cuba that had underlying economic interests. According to Normando, Spain had accepted him and a scant number of other political prisoners from Cuba as part of a campaign the Ministry of Foreign Affairs and Cooperation had been waging to persuade the European Union to remove the Common Position[3] that had been imposed on Cuba for

3 As reported by the BBC on October 25, 2010: "The EU's 'common position,' dating back to 1996, demands that Cuba makes progress on democracy and human rights before any normalization of ties."

nearly a decade. Although the Spanish government had trumpeted Cuba's move as evidence of a shift in their position on human rights, Normando and his brothers-in-arms saw it as exile—pawns in a greater political plotline. Once in Spain, the exiles were only granted the bare minimum: basic shelter, a meal allowance, and a limited travel expense. The Spanish ministry refused to give the ex-prisoners any refugee status, or rights to work, or travel privileges (at least that would facilitate being able to talk about their experiences in Cuban jails); and, as this paper that the translator held revealed, the ministry could withhold anything at will. As Normando had said earlier into the tape recorder, "*Libre pero no gratuito*." The document showed the food allowance had been reduced by about ten percent this month. And the travel line had been completely eliminated. The translator was working that out with some officials later in the week, but until then, Normando and his wife were grounded.

We left all our Metro tickets on the table. We'd buy more at the subway station. In our case it was just a matter of inconvenience.

Before leaving, we asked the translator what else they needed. He said clothes for the little girl. She'd already outgrown what was donated. That night we went out and bought Daniela clothes, as well as art supplies, and a notebook for writing poetry—something Normando had said she was very interested in. We gave them to him the next day. Initially, Normando refused the items, seeing them as charity. "They are for Daniela," we insisted. "A birthday gift." She had recently turned nine.

* * *

Later in the week, Normando looked tired. One afternoon, when he stepped out of the living room, his wife, Yaraí, explained that our previous day's talks had brought back so much, causing him to toss-and-turn in night terrors. Coming back in, Normando announced it didn't matter. The story needs to be told. We were glad to be part of it.

—Adam Braver & Molly Gessford

NORMANDO HERNÁNDEZ GONZÁLEZ:

7 Years in Prison for Writing About Bread

PART ONE

An Entirely Negative Force

1.

I always thought I would die. Always. From the moment one is involved in these things in Cuba, even if it is through passive means, you will always fear for your life.

2.

During March of 2000, in what is now known internationally as the Black Spring, the Cuban government initiated a witch-hunt all over the island. They systematically targeted independent journalists who, through peaceful opposition, fought for the rights and liberties of our people.

In Cuba, independent newspapers do not exist. The government has full control of printing presses. It's an exclusive monopoly. Article 53 of the Republic of Cuba's constitution actually states that any activity that is fundamentally aligned with free speech and independent presses is illegal; it only respects the liberty of expression and presses in accordance with the ideologies of the government.

That spring, I'd been working as the director of the Independent Journalists Association of Camagüey (*el Colegio de Periodistas Independientes de Camagüey*). Our stated objective, through unorthodox means, was to break the silence in the Midwest region of Cuba about what was happening in our country, bringing to light existing violence, as well as general information. Such principles led us to creating the magazine *Luz Cubana*, a socio-cultural journal on Cuban life.

The risks were understood. We knew Cuban law did not permit us to do this, but, as our apostle Jose Martí once said, the only thing unfair laws are good for is to be violated. Especially when they are laws against the principles and dignity of human beings.

Within a matter of weeks, there would be a military operation in which the government arrested over one hundred independent journalists.

Seventy-five of us would be tried and sentenced and jailed.

3.

On March 18th, I was traveling back home to Vertientes in Camagüey. I was coming from Havana, where I'd been doing a trial-run printing of *Luz Cubana*. In the waiting area of the Omnibus terminal, the television showed members of the Cuban government having a round-table discussion, railing against the Cuban civil society. It wasn't just what they were saying that caught my attention—it was their tone. Something really bad was happening. You could tell. Still, at that point, I had no clue what was to come.

I'd only wanted to get home to see my wife, Yaraí, and our baby daughter, Daniela, who was just four days shy of her first birthday.

4.

My bus finally reached Vertientes around five in the morning. Exhausted, I slept into the morning, until 9:30, when the persistently ringing phone finally got me out of bed.

It was the Radio Martí[4] journalist, Efren Martinez Pulgarón, phoning from Florida.

Hearing my voice, Efren said he was surprised that *I* had not yet been arrested.

Arrested?

He then proceeded to tell me about the wave of violent arrests occurring throughout the island.

Don't forget: I was a journalist. Immediately after that phone call, I began contacting reporters from the association that I directed. We needed to verify Efren's information about the arrests that had already happened in Camagüey. They were already on it. It was true. People were being taken from their homes. The reporters had names. Locations. Witnesses.

We passed that information along to Radio Martí.

Then, together, we started contacting all the international journalists that we knew, telling them what was going on, hoping they would tell the world.

4 A U.S.-backed station based in Florida that broadcasts Spanish reports to Cuba.

5.

By mid-morning, family and friends began arriving at my house. A strange operation was under way in Vertientes, they warned. The police department was full of people and vehicles from out of town.

They were preparing to arrest me.

Grabbing my little girl, I jumped on my bicycle. And I just started riding. Touring around the city, it all unfolded before my eyes. The United National Revolutionary Police office had swelled with military vehicles and high-ranking officials. And so too had the Department of State Security. Uniformed policemen. Plainclothes policemen. Soldiers and officers. Everything was so still. In that moment, I can't say I was conscious of my actions. But unconsciously, I was going to say goodbye to my close friends and family.

6.

The first vehicles began approaching at three in the afternoon. Rumbling up my street. I was in my backyard feeding my daughter a popsicle while she sat in her playpen. Their cars braked suddenly and loudly, screeching to a stop in front of my house. My next-door neighbor came out running. "Normandito!" she called. "Normandito! Run! Run! Run! Run, the police are here!"

I was prepared—at least I thought I was prepared—to be arrested, especially knowing everything that was going on in Cuba at the time. But I still panicked. I dropped the popsicle down on the chair. And I ran.

I dashed across my patio, crossing over into my neighbor's yard, where he was cooking slop in a large pot on the ground, the customary food for pigs in Cuba. Next to him, there was a forty-year-old mango tree. I headed straight for it. The mango tree's trunk was so thick that I could barely climb up to the first branch without his help. But I made it, thanks to him. And that was where I hid.

From the heights of the tree, I watched them comb the area. They set up a command post at a school behind my house. Armed police officers with handguns climbed atop my neighbor's roof. Military officials were taking over my neighborhood.

Tracking dogs made their way across the yard. Miraculously, the animals stopped just before the trunk of the tree, suddenly confused. It turned out that the lighter fluid that my neighbor had used for firewood to cook the pig slop killed the scent. The police looked up, right into the branches.

I can't say it was *just* a coincidence that they didn't see me, it was a coincidence at the hands of God who wanted me to be at my little girl's side on her first birthday.

7.

At 9:30 PM, when the last vehicle left, I climbed down from the tree and jogged home. Inside my house were my sister, my uncles, my wife, and my brother-in-law. I told them to lock the front door, and we sat in the living room to talk. Before long, we heard another police car arrive with more dogs.

I immediately ran upstairs and hid under the bed.

The police asked Yaraí for one of my baseball hats. They let the dogs sniff it and then set them loose. Of course, they smelled me everywhere—it *was* my house! Realizing this search would be fruitless, the police left after a few minutes.

I ended up hiding under the bed for six days, until March 24th. Those were days filled with desperation.

8.

On different occasions, in the middle of the night, the police attempted to open our bedroom windows. I could hear the shuffling of the guards as they changed shifts outside my house.

During this time, my wife was harassed, pressured, and threatened for her life.

They also threatened to take away our daughter, because, as they saw it, she was a child of the revolution.

They said they would demolish our home; and, because our house is on a large plot of land, they told my wife that they were going to turn our home into a park for children.

There was always, always, an entirely negative force.

9.

I would go under the bed at six in the morning.

During the day I'd listen to Radio Martí, Radio Francia Internacional, Radio Netherland, and La Vos de la Americas. They'd report what was happening in Cuba; the whole world was criticizing the Cuban government. I heard live interviews with my mom, and interviews with my wife in my house. And my mother would be sobbing by the end. And my wife would be sobbing by the end.

I'd come out at eleven at night.

After taking a shower, I would eat with Yaraí, go upstairs into Daniela's room, and just watch her sleep in her crib. Then I'd kiss her goodnight and climb into my marriage bed with Yaraí.

At six in the morning, I'd slip down to the floor, returning to my hiding place under the bed.

I knew this couldn't last, that eventually I was going to have to turn myself in. But I told myself I wouldn't do it until after my little girl turned one.

10.

On the afternoon of my daughter's birthday, decorations already had been put up. Daniela was playing in back with her grandmother, aunt, uncle, and cousin. No one knew I was hiding under the bed, other than Yaraí's mother. We'd made excuses for my absence. The Cuban government traditionally responds to those who oppose them either by jailing, shooting, or forcing them into exile. This treatment can extend to the closest family members. We didn't want trouble for anyone.

But then came a knock on the door.

From the living room, Yaraí called out, "Who is it?"

"Yellow Fever Prevention Company." Their voices were unnaturally deep. "Just here for an inspection," they said. It was obvious they were military personnel disguised as exterminators, pretending to represent the government's mosquito abatement campaign, a program that granted full access into homes.

"Then go around to the back walkway," she instructed them. "That's where you'll find the water containers."

"Are you hiding something in the house? Is that why you don't want us to walk through the house?"

From under the bed I heard everything.

"No, no, no," Yaraí said, thinking quickly, trying to quash their suspicions. "Wait one minute, don't go." Opening the door, she put on a calm, welcoming voice: "If what you are interested in is searching my home, then search it." They came in without hesitation, outfitted in exterminator uniforms but wearing dress shoes. Yaraí took them throughout the bottom floor of our house. They moved quickly. You could hear their breaths almost sighing in disappointment at seeing nothing other than birthday decorations and empty furniture. Occasionally a closet door would open. A cabinet banging shut.

As though it were nothing, she led them upstairs. The soles of their shoes squeaked on each step. "And here," she said from the landing, loud enough to make sure I heard, "is the bedroom." She partially blocked the threshold.

In those moments you don't think about anything.

In those moments your heart feels like it is going to jump out of your throat.

And in those moments you just wait for the worst.

They coughed. Paused. Looked past her into the room. "We really should check all standing water," one of them finally said, still trying to keep up the charade of being exterminators. "Do you have any religious rituals that require you to place cups of water in the wardrobe or, say, under the bed?"

"As I've said, if your objective is to search my house, then, please, search it!" With her back to the bed, Yaraí flung open the wardrobe doors. Calmly and deliberately she turned around, and took two steps in. You could hear the hinges on the wardrobe doors still squeaking. The men moved with her. I was watching them, their polished leather shoes—their feet were right there in front of me. Right there! Inches from me.

Yaraí bent forward, and, like the final step in a magician's trick, she yanked up our comforter, revealing nothing but sheets and pillows.

I held my breath under the bed, curled like a knot against the wall.

11.

It's important to point out this detail I forgot to mention: when I was hiding, they spread information throughout the neighborhood—and the city, for that matter—that they were looking for me, claiming I had a bomb that I was going to plant in an elementary school. They were circulating a photograph of me, a large photo, and were showing it to everyone. They searched cars. They searched everywhere. Searched everything.

12.

I can't stop myself from thinking of this incredible detail: the solidarity of my friends and my family. At the time of the arrests, I didn't have, as the Cuban's say, a single *pido predo*; I didn't have even one peso. I had invested my money in my daughter's birthday and in the magazine, which was a huge expense for me. When my friends became aware of the situation, they gave my wife money. They even brought her food.

13.

I lived in fear. At any moment, I could be arrested. After taking an inner journey, I concluded that if I were arrested and sentenced to jail, then I would have to go. I would not be the first nor the last person to go to prison for defending his beliefs. What I had to do was stick to my convictions. I had to retain my principles. I could not allow them to destroy me—especially not like they were at that time. And I made up an adage for myself: *I don't have to worry about anything because I have done nothing detrimental against humanity*. It was the state who were the ones doing wrong. And since I did not have a guilty conscious then there was nothing to fear. To tell you the truth, from that moment on I was filled with a spiritual peace. Despite the difficulties that would continue to present themselves, I felt much stronger after that. Much stronger.

14.

Even after Yaraí convinced the men to leave, I didn't come out. Even as I heard Daniela's birthday party going on downstairs, I didn't come out.

At the safe hour of eleven, I crept into Daniela's room. She was snuggled in her crib. The house was quiet. The streets silent, the military vehicles shut down for the night. I leaned over to listen to her sleep. Her breath was warm and almost milky smelling. I kissed her cheek; caressed her head. Tomorrow morning, she'd wake up as a one-year-old. And I would celebrate that with her. She would know her papa's birthday kiss. And how much I loved her. And how much a part of her I was. That could never be taken from us. But by tomorrow evening, I would sit with my wife, my sister, and my uncle. I would tell them this cat-and-mouse game couldn't go on forever. It wasn't good for anybody. I would give my sister a letter to deliver to the head of the state police, telling him I would surrender peacefully in my home. At least, it would be over.

Sitting beside my little girl, I cried silently, choking on tears of blood, stroking her face and watching her sleep peacefully in her world, still untouched by fear.

15.

Adam Braver: Was there a specific moment when you came to the realization that you couldn't go on hiding?

Normando Hernández González: No, no. It was simple. I had to turn myself in. I was going to turn myself in because I had no reason to run.

Molly Gessford: Could you have run?

Normando: Actually, a few of my friends brought me an outfit: a wig and a woman's dress. They wanted to disguise me in order to get me out of the house, to give me a chance to get away so these people wouldn't find me. But no, I declined all of this.

16.

Back in '94, when I was at university (teaching technology at *el Instituto Politécnico Cruce de la Trocha*, and also studying construction engineering at *el Instituto Superior Pedagógico José Martí*), I didn't know anything about politics. I was born straight into propaganda. The only information I had about the world was information completely distorted by the perspective of the only political party that exists in Cuba. And when I saw the dedicated patriotism of my friends, the unquestioning patriotism of all the Cuban people, doubts always surged in me.

Well, I'd wonder, is it me who is wrong, or is it the majority that is wrong?

Around that time, I discovered the Universal Declaration of Human Rights. It was as if it landed right into my hands. Reading it led me to even more questioning—particularly in the area of free expression, and the type of struggle it would take to defend our basic rights as human beings. In fact, one of my first "jobs" as a dissident in Cuba was to distribute the Universal Declaration of Human Rights to my fellow Cubans. Many family and friends would say, "Don't you see the consequences of asking all these questions?" (I suppose they were right, as the moment I began question to my political world, the universities expelled me for alleged ideological problems, in particular, "dissenting from the policy of the Cuban government.") "What is it that you want?" they'd ask. "What is it that you are searching for?"

"The simple act of having your rights to liberty and expression," I would say. "The simple act of not being scared to say what you are thinking."

17.

In Cuba we have a saying, "*If I get out of this one, I've got a brujo,*" referring to a sacred form of witchcraft adopted from the Africana religions that have influenced our culture.

That first morning, when I'd ridden my bicycle with Daniela to say my goodbyes, I found myself talking with that sense of humor that is characteristic of Cubans. "If I get out of this one," I'd say to each friend, "I've got a *brujo* on my side."

It was the only thing I could think of to tell them. And then I'd ride off, my daughter with me, pedaling slowly, believing I had at least enough magic—enough of a *brujo*—behind me to see her through her first year of life.

18.

Braver: Was it a scene when the police finally came to take you away?

Normando: No, it was passive. I had set conditions before I would allow them to arrive at my home. And, frankly, my terms were advantegous to the police, as well. They knew the people in my neighborhood adored me. The police knew that if they came with an outrageous operation that I would find it aggressive and resist arrest. They knew they would not be able to control the situation if it got to that point, especially not with my family and neighbors at my side. And that's why they agreed to do what I told them.

Gessford: Which was?

Normando: One official, one car.

Gessford: And so what happens that morning?

Normando: The official arrives on time in an old Russian car, knocking on my front door. I answer it, carrying my daughter. It's almost silent. Nothing is spoken. Everything is understood. Daniela starts to cry as I hand her off to her mother. But I just stand straight. Ready to march on.

Braver: What's going through your mind?

Normando: Oddly, I feel very calm. Maybe because I can sense that my family and my neighbors are more scared than I am. Maybe because I can see they need me to reflect strength and assurance.

Gessford: And the official?

Normando: Quiet and stoic.

Gessford: What images do you remember in those last moments?

Normando: I see my neighbors standing in their homes and in the street, saluting and blowing kisses. But I also see the worry and fear in their faces.

Braver: And where are you taken?

Normando: Straight to the state security office for the province of Camagüey, where I will be held in a very small cell that doesn't even have one meter of free space, sealed with an iron wall and another very dark wood door.

PART TWO

I Am No Common Criminal

1.

A small incandescent bulb was lit twenty-four hours a day. The suffocating heat made you feel always on the verge of asphyxiation.

The toilet was so filthy, filthy, filthy. Maggots lived inside it. A simple hole would have been better.

Dirty water came from a pipe near the toilet; supposedly my drinking water. It was only turned on once a day, running for no more than ten to fifteen minutes.

The small bed, constructed of metal and wire, had a mattress made of a nylon sack filled with a dried herb call malagueta. The bedding was black, like the dirt left on your hands after digging in the dirt. But now imagine that all over your arms and clothes, that's what laying on top of the mattress felt like. As though it had transferred all its filth to you.

I was in this cell for a few days, sharing it with a delinquent accused of drug trafficking.

Later, they transferred me to a bigger cell. But that only meant living with more delinquents.

2.

Braver: Did you know what every step was going to be? Did you even know if you would have a trial?

Normando: Yes, I was completely aware. Those nights hiding under the bed—listening to the foreign radio stations—had given me a handle on what was going on around the island with the others who'd been arrested. In fact, I had a conversation with my wife, my sister, and my uncle the night before I turned myself in. I spoke candidly: *I am sure I will be sentenced to no less than twenty years in prison. But taking into account the international campaign, and how it has developed against the government because of these arrests, I don't think I will even serve five years.*

But I was wrong.

Eleven days after I turned myself in, in the middle of the night, I received a petition from the public attorney that asked for a sanction of life in prison, which, in Cuba, is next in line to the death penalty.

Braver: Was that sanction true for all the arrested journalists, or just for you?

Normando: It was applied to a small group of us out of the seventy-five. I had thought they were going to execute many people from the people in our group.

Gessford: Why do you think that was done? Was this punishment for people who were perceived to have higher profiles?

Normando: I don't think so. I mean, among us, Raúl Rivero had at one point worked for the government; Marta Beatriz Roque was well known and popular—both were leaders who had gained lots of national and international recognition. Nevertheless they were sentenced to only twenty years in prison.

And you ask why was this done? To cause disagreements between us. But that's something they were never able to accomplish.

3.

The night before the trial I was sent a gray prisoner's uniform to wear.

Initally, I accepted the package. Later, the guards came back to make sure I'd actually put it on. I'd been waiting for them. When they opened the small window to my cell to check, I threw the bundle of clothes through the opening. I yelled in protest, "I am no common criminal. I haven't been convicted of any crime yet, so I should not be expected to dress like a prisoner." I carried this on for a while, so inspired that by the time I finally finished I'd almost lost my voice. And all the other prisoners that were being held there—the common criminals—began applauding.

But it wasn't over. In the early morning hours, around 6:00 AM, two burly men over six feet tall took me from my cell to a small room. There, prison officials were waiting for me. The two men lifted me up. I started to scream, hoping my calls might be heard down in the cells. One slapped his hand over my mouth. The other then stripped off my clothes, forcing me limb by limb into the prisoner's uniform.

4.

Gessford: Just to clarify: you didn't wear the clothes because you didn't believe you should be identified as a common prisoner?

Normando: I was a prisoner of conscience as declared by Amnesty International. A stipulation of that designation is that the prisoner of conscience has to be differentiated from the common population of the prison. But in order for the government to demoralize, degrade, and destroy us—both physically and morally—they mixed us with all the common delinquents and criminals on the very first day we entered the prison. And so the only way we could differentiate ourselves was to not dress the same as them.

And it was also a form of protest.

5.

Every Wednesday, I got to see Yaraí in person. I can't remember if we were granted five minutes or fifteen minutes; it wasn't much. However, when I was with Yaraí, it seemed like time never ran out. The visits took place in a tiny room with an officer from the state security standing guard. It was hard to talk about anything substantial. We were simply expected to say good morning and eat a snack. The first thing I always asked was how our daughter was doing, how my mother was. But if I tried to discuss anything related to the case against me, the guard would interrupt us. If I pressed on, the guard simply declared the visit was over.

6.

I always talked. If I had the desire to speak, I spoke.

7.

The trial was on the twelfth day. From Camagüey, four of us were taken to our proceedings at the same time, moved in patrol cars on the highway with motorcycle cops leading the way, sirens on. We were dressed in the uniforms. Once again, they had forced us into them.

It was a closed hearing, which only allowed two family members to enter the courtroom, in this case my wife and my father. Still, the courtroom was jammed. There were news cameras. The seating area was full of people (including a friend of mine who was able to sneak in. My wife's parents were also able to get in because Yaraí's father is a judge).

There was one judge and two lay judges. Lay judges, elected by the people, only assist because they have not yet completed the requirements to be a judge. But all are supposed to have high morals and a variety of principles. And to be part of the communist party.

8.

One of the first witnesseses for the prosecution was a supposed agent from the state security. The judge asked him what kind of journalism I did, and what specifically were the concerns.

"He has criticized the quality of bread."

9.

Gessford: Why did they focus on the article about the bread?

Normando: While I wrote about many things, bread was the main piece of evidence against me at trial. Even though, in his testimony, the official from the state security acknowledged the quality of bread was not good, still he claimed that I created a commotion by blaming the Cuban government for the poor quality of the bread.

Gessford: Did the prosecution bother to look for other infractions to charge you with?

Normando: Certainly. They searched my home from three in the afternoon until nine at night, but they found nothing other than some magazines, the Universal Declaration of Human Rights, a short wave radio, a fax machine I had actually bought from the Cuban government, a Remington typewriter from WWII, and over 40 books of journalism. The bread was the best they could come up with.

Gessford: So you were tried over bread?

Normando: I was being punished for my part in supporting and developing independent journalism that did not exist within the parameters of the Cuban government.

10.

At the trial, the prosecution retierated its request that I should be sentenced to life in prison for the severity of the crimes I had committed as a journalist.

11.

The day after the hearing, the judge and his secretary came to meet with me in the holding room. He said my sentence was twenty-five years-to-life. Very calmly, I thanked him for not not making it a life sentence. The judge just stared at me. I could see what he was thinking: *twenty-five years-to-life and life in prison are the same thing.*

12.

They sent me to the state security offices with one of the other brothers of the cause who had been sentenced with me. This was a temporary cell, a transit site. One where the beds were concrete slabs. With cement walls that were built with a prickly texture to prevent you from leaning against them. The drinking water pipe went directly into the hole that we used for our bathroom needs.

13.

For three consecutive nights they transferred me to a hospital, in which there was an office filled with multiple disciplinary psychologists and psychiatrists. I was examined. Evaluated for signs of mental illness. A psychological review—the kind that's typically only done when someone has been sentenced to death by firing squad.

14.

Braver: You believed you could be shot?

Normando: Of course. Of course.

PART THREE

Only a Fraction Compared to the Reality

1.

And there I was able to see for the first time what I had been told about the special regimes of Cuban prisons.

2.

Braver: Let's talk about being in prison.

3.

Following the trials, the prisoners of conscience were moved from the the western part of the country to the eastern. And vice-versa. The entire country was involved: the center and both sides of the island. The seven of us from the Camagüey sweeps were moved to Santiago de Cuba, about five hundred miles away from my home. At the time we didn't know where we were going. We didn't even know we were to be moved. We had no idea where they were taking us.

4.

We were taken on a bus typically used for tourists, and next to each of us, seated separately, sat an official from the State Security Department wearing a bullet proof vest and all his weapons. This bus was escorted by police cars, motorcycles, and ambulances. There were many Russian cars—those were the ones used at that time by the state security of Cuba. We were not allowed to talk amongst ourselves. For the entire trip, we couldn't even open the curtains to look outside.

They drove in the middle of the road. Oncoming traffic had to pull off to the sides to get out of the way. Upon entering each province, the next motorized brigade in charge would be waiting for us at the entrance. They then became responsible for our caravan. Then they would lead us through the province to meet the next motorized brigade waiting at the other end.

5.

Normando: We arrived at a prison in Santiago de Cuba in the early morning hours before dawn. Boniato Prison. And within Boniato we would be housed in the special area known as Boniatico, reserved for the most hardened and dangerous criminals. Once we pulled in, they called my name and told me to get off the bus. I was going to stay there.

Gessford: Just you?

Normando: No, I stayed there with other brothers of the cause. Another journalist named Juan Carlos Vera Costa was already there serving his time. There were seven of us.

Gessford: Had they told you anything else yet?

Normando: Nothing was said until we were inside. There a guard told us, "You are about to enter a severe place. Do not get close to any jail cell even if a prisoner calls you. Just walk through the center of the aisle." As I said, the inmates there were highly dangerous. Boniatico was for those who had been sentenced to life in prison and the death penalty.

Gessford: So these were all common criminals?

Normando: Murderers. Maniacs. Very bad people.

6.

It was my first look at what a prison was really like. At that moment, an American movie came to mind, *Bad Boys*. I remembered the star of the movie walking into a prison very similar to the one we were entering. But there was one main difference: in the movie there wasn't an immediate threat posed by the prisoners.

7.

Braver: So you felt the threat of physical violence?

Normando: Yes, there you could even be killed. There were people with illnesses, many with HIV and AIDS. There were murderers who were completely mentally alienated, the types who saw wrongdoing as an accomplishment.

That prisoners slept during the day and created nocturnal lives, simply because they feared the night.

It was four o'clock in the morning when we arrived. With the noise inside the prison, you would've thought it was twelve o'clock in the afternoon.

Immediately, the inmates began questioning us, wanting to know who we were. So we began to tell them. As it happened, some of these were condemned prisoners, having been sentenced to death by firing squad. And previously we had led campaigns in Cuba to annul their very sentences. When they realized who we were, I remember seeing the jubilee in their expressions. They began yelling, "Oi! These are the defenders of human rights, the ones who ran the campaign against death by firing squad."

Gessford: So then you felt safer among the other prisoners?

Normando: Absolutely not. Remember, that was the first night we arrived; that same man who had welcomed us with such jubilee, later became our worst enemy in the prison. These people are insane, how they act depends on how they wake up that day—they either give you everything or they kill you.

8.

My first taste of the daily breakfast. I will never forget it! It was like something we call *chorrote*—like the food we feed pigs—made up of cornmeal boiled in water.

I thought the *charrote* was being served cold, but when I went to drink from the cup, I burned the inside of my mouth—the slop was still boiling. We were also given a piece of bread, so small it looked like a box of matches. "The Matchbox"—that's how the prisoners referred to the bread. And they put me in jail for commenting about its quality?

The *borundanga* was made up of the most visceral meat—you could see the hide, the hair, and there was even feces in there. The guards who served us would put a handkerchief over their faces because the odor coming from the food was unbearable. There was another meal, a tench dish, famous in Cuba for its fishy smell. They gave it to us rotten and boiled, and due to the amount of fish bones, it looked like a magnet full of pins. Because they used the same serving spoon, everything tasted of tench.

After we protested, they did change our breakfast—exchanging the *chorrote* for cereal (although that was like drinking water with sawdust; it actually scratched your throat).

The only thing I ate was bread. But that had to be purchased from the common prisoners. One small piece cost five cigarettes. Although I didn't smoke, I knew cigarettes were like money inside the prison. My friends made sure to send many cartons with my wife when she visited. With this banked currency, I could buy bread for myself, as well as get it to my brothers in the cause, so they too could eat a little. Because no one could eat that food.

9.

After being there there for several months, my brothers and I began to protest in order to improve the living conditions. We had some successes. They changed the mattresses. They provided more serving spoons for meal times so that our food would not be contaminated. The little red worms and other harmful materials were cleaned out of the water tanks. We convinced them to install speakers so that we could finally listen to the radio, and every once in a while, we were able to listen to the news. But, most importantly, we succeeded in getting a phone that we could use. Still, even with those changes, everything pretty much remained the same. The abuse and mistreatment of the prisoners was still horrible.

10.

My only sunlight hours were Monday through Friday at noon. In the eastern part of the country, it is the worst kind of heat. It gave me a heat rash all over my body.

11.

At eleven in the morning, the official from the state security arrives with the head of the area where I've been placed. Just for context, this semi-illiterate man had led a platoon during the era when they still assassinated people in Cuba. And it was with him that I would have my first confrontation with a prison official. He enters my cell, stands in front of me, and begins to insult me. I react. Defend myself. And then I let him have it, telling him everything I think about him—and his mother. I was moved to another cell, the worst cell in the special regime.

12.

A big role in our decision to go on a hunger strike ocurred on August 13th. It was Fidel Castro's birthday, and, at around 9:00 PM, I was in my cell conversing with the prisoner next door. A guard passing by told me to lay down, and to "stop talking shit." He called me a counterrevolutionary, a mercenary. In that moment, I let my brother, Manuel Vázquez Portal, who was on the opposite side of the cell, know what was going on. We were always separated, and we never saw each other. The only way we could communicate was through yelling.

Manuel called to the guard, "HEY! HEY! Normando is not alone here, his brothers are here too." And then all the brothers of the cause began to protest too. We began to give a speech to the entire population, speaking loudly, coalescing our individual voices into a single, unified voice that basically said, "How is it that prisoners are denied their human rights? You *can* defend youselves." We just couldn't stand to see such injustices prevailing.

Seven of us gave speech after speech. When one tired, another would continue. After each speech, all the prisoners would pound on the doors, on the locks. "Long live human rights!" we'd chant as a choir. "Out with Fidel! Out with Communism!"

We protested until three in the morning. And then we demanded an audience with the provincial director of the jails and prisons. The guards mobilized, standing by with dogs. They were scared to see all of us so infuriated, especially the common prisoners.

In calling for a meeting with the director, we wanted to make the case that he should provide light in the cells. Others, on my behalf, argued that I should be moved out of my cell. It was the only cell completely sealed and dark.

But despite all our demands, and all our protests, the director refused to come.

13.

Two days later, state security officials took me into an office. For my disobedience on the thirteenth, they were taking away my conjugal visits. "My supposed disobedience was provoked by you," I responded. "Plus, my conjugal visits are a regulated right that you can't violate." If they took away those visits, I said, I would be forced to take a stand. A hunger strike.

The state security had the same conversations with with Manuel Vázquez Portal and Nelson Adiar. My two brothers of the cause answered exactly as I did. As per usual, they only penalized three out of our seven brothers, hoping to create a wedge. And again, to no effect. All seven of us remained in solidarity.

14.

They knew we were serious. In order to stem our plans, a state security officer told us they'd decided to return our conjugal visits; therefore we no longer had a reason to go on strike. The seven of us voted on whether we should proceed with the strike. I argued that we should not go on strike at this time because we had won on the issue of conjugal visits, giving us some momentum to keep fighting. Others contended that this was about more than conjugal visits, but about all of our rights being violated. It was about the totality of our demands, and, fundamentally, the provincial director's refusal to speak with us.

We voted democratically. The majority voted in favor of striking, four to three.

It was agreed that we would begin the hunger strike after we had our last visitations. Mine was scheduled as the second to last, to be followed by Manuel Vásquez Portal.

Once Manuel returned from his visitation, we began our hunger strike on the thirtieth of August.

15.

In Cuba, when you say you're going on a hunger strike, the first thing the officers do is strip you of all of your belongings. When the guards came for my things, I said, "Hey, I refused my food, I did not refuse my clothes." But they took everything, including the mattress from the bed. All they left me was my underwear.

16.

After four days of being on strike, I was rustled out of my cell at 6:00 AM. The guards said I needed to be tranferred because I was the leader of the demonstration and strike. I was interred in a completely sealed police patrol car with two security guards: one from the state, another from the prisons and jails. I was crammed into the middle of the backseat, forced to sit on the plastic wedge between the seats. I sat there handcuffed with a bucket between my legs. Pressed between the two guards, I could only support myself against the motion of the vehicle by leaning my forehead against the acrylic sheet that separated the back of the patrol car from the driver's area.

I experienced a lot of nausea. My overall health was weak in general; it was beginning to go downhill. Even before the hunger strike, I'd only eaten eight times that month of August. I just couldn't stomach the food.

The patrol car stopped in Ciego de Avila for lunch. The officers also wanted a medic to check me out. But I wouldn't accept any of their care. I wouldn't permit any medics to take my vital signs, nor did I eat food. I only drank water.

17.

On the long ride, I was thinking thousands of things—first and foremost that I would not make it alive to wherever I was going. I felt my life slipping away, little by little.

18.

After some seventeen hours, at 11:00 PM, we arrived at Pinar del Río, a prison on the westernmost province in Cuba.

19.

The prison in Pinar del Río has three different areas. *Area One* is for the most severe prisoners; *Area Two* holds the less severe inmates; and *Area Three* incarcerates juveniles.

In the morning, they took me out of *Area One* of the prison, which was where I had arrived, and then took me to the dungeons of *Area Three*. There, they put me to live with only a pair of shorts, a T-shirt, a toothbrush, and toothpaste. There was no water. Only the liter-and-a-half they brought daily. From that cell, I was determined to continue my hunger strike.

20.

A *turco* is a trench where people relieve themselves that goes through the prison; it ran right down the middle my new cell, shallow with a small cement wall. It was filled with urine.

21.

I didn't have any water, and there was no light. The cell was completely closed off, boarded up. There was a small crack at the top of the door. If I stood on four or five books, I was able to look out into the prison.

The mosquitoes' hunger increased at night, making it that much harder to rest. There was not an inch of me without a mosquito bite. Small red balls. On every, every, every, every, every part of my body.

22.

The rats used the *turcos* to move throughout the prison, entering and exiting through our cells. The *turco* was less than a yard away from my bed and at about the same height. I slept with my feet facing the *turco*; my head in the opposite direction. In the middle of my first night, I felt something cold and sticky jump near my foot. A rat was crawling across my body. Instinctively, I started to jump up and down. I didn't know what was in the cell with me, my room was completely dark, sealed off, only the prisoners were up then. The rat tumbled to the floor, escaping under the cell door. I could hear prisoners cheering as the rat ran through the corridor. That's how many prisoners entertained themselves—trying to catch rats. The game was that when a rat came into a cell, then the person inside that cell would scare it into another cell. This would continue on and on, until the rat found itself in front of someone waiting for it. The end of the line.

I spent forty-eight hours without being allowed to shower, unable to get rid of the lingering smell of the rat. No matter how much I yelled and protested, the guards wouldn't take me to shower.

I never could sleep in that cell.

23.

The guards did not care about any of this, mostly because they did not know me. Also the officials from state security told them that I was a terrorist. They had even said that to the common prisoners in the area. They tried to tell that to just about the entire world. That I was a terrorist.

24.

To get through something like this, you think about your family. You think about the fact that you have a little girl who needs you, and you think about your wife and your mother. You think about the entire community which has confidence in you, the people who believe in you. It all serves to give you enough strength to push forward, and to tolerate and overcome all these horrible situations. It also helps to know that many brothers walked before us—many before I was born; they fought for the same causes, and went through the same abuses and mistreatments, and knew the same tortures. Knowing this gave me strength. If they could do it, why would I not be able to? I am a person just like they were. You see, we were experiencing first hand what we had been fighting against, what we had been denouncing for years. That desire to continue working for the cause kept all of us strong.

25.

Braver: What did Yaraí know? Did she know where you were?

Normando: No. On the last visitation we had at Boniato, just before the hunger strike got underway, I had said, "Go to Havana. Tell them what's happened to us here. Why we've been sentenced. Show the whole world, so everyone knows why I've been punished." At the time I was being moved, she was on her way to Havana.

Before leaving Santiago de Cuba, I yelled to my brothers, "They're taking me! And I do not know where they are taking me! Get in touch with my wife. Tell her that they are going to make me vanish. Disappear!" That was the only way my wife could find out what was happening. In fact, a few days later, worried about me, she called the prison to check in on me. At this point, I was already at Pinar del Río, hundreds and hundreds miles away. But the officials in Santiago de Cuba lied, telling her, "Yes, he is fine, he is fine." Shortly thereafter, Yaraí began to figure out I wasn't in Boniato anymore. However, she had no idea where I was, or, for that matter, if I was still even alive. And despite whenever she went for information, there wasn't a single official who would tell her where I was. Seven or eight days after I was transferred, one of the inmates who heard my plea called Yaraí, letting her know I'd beeen transferred. With that bit of information, she was able to pressure the authorties into telling her where I was.

26.

It was my tenth day at Pinar del Río. The guards summoned me. They said there was a visitor. Along with her father, Yaraí had travelled from Camagüey to my new home. I could not walk. I barely had the strength to talk. I could barely breathe. The guards had to carry me up to the visiting room. That alone must have been torture for them. Before I went on the hunger strike, the prison officials had not let me shower for three days. By now, it had come close to eighteen days. From the inside out, I was completely filthy.

27.

I believe that was my wife's saddest experience. She doesn't even like to speak of it—of when they let her see me.

28.

To be honest, when I was still a journalist—before I was imprisoned—my sources told me about the things occurring inside the prisons. Some I was able to verify and publish; others I could not. There were some reports that made me skeptical. I thought they must be exaggerating. But once I experienced it in the flesh, once I lived in that suffering, I realized what had been said about prisons was only a fraction compared to the reality of the situation.

29.

Braver: Did you have any sense of what was happening to the other seventy-four journalists during this time?

Normando: One thing should be noted: among the seventy-five of us arrested during the Black Spring, very few of us actually knew each other. I met many of them for the first time inside the prisons. Others I didn't even meet until I was exiled here in Madrid.

Braver: Yet you managed to create a connection with many of them, even when you were held in different prisons, in different parts of the country.

Normando: Most news was communicated through conjugal visits and through telephone calls. Through those processes, more or less we stayed informed about each other's predicaments: who was on a hunger strike, who had suffered torture. But most importantly, we always stayed in solidarity. If any one of us seventy-five had a problem, even when we didn't know each other, we would go on a hunger strike, we would protest, we would support that person. We were all part of the same cause.

Braver: So through your network you were able to stand together on your positions?

Normando: Exactly. So for example, there was one particular case when Raúl Castro made a proposal to the U.S. to exchange the seventy-five of us for five spies. We protested inside the jail, demanding they not make the exchange. We hardly even needed any contact to reach communal agreements. In short, our response to anything the Cuban government wanted to do was almost always: *No.*

It was very important that no one succumbed. All of us remained firm. We could not be destroyed, especially not those of us with high morals and a lot of integrity. (Of course, there were those who couldn't withstand the pressure, which we understood—after all we are human beings.) But it quickly became clear that they would not able to destroy us as easily as they anticipated.

30.

In Pinar del Río, I also refused to wear the uniform. For that I was punished by being sent to solitary confinement for one hundred and one days.

31.

My cell was 85cm wide x 125 cm long. There was barely any room to move—the *turco* and bed took up nearly all of the space. Just me and the rats. But this only covers the first two prisons. I would be moved again. And again. And again. By the end, I would see and know the vicious workings of four prisons.

PART FOUR

We Can Kill You and Nothing Will Happen

1.

The first time I was physically mistreated, my first instance of physical aggression, was in Pinar del Río. There, a re-educator named Ryanair Pulgaron threw me down some stairs. Ryanair and two other guards dragged me across the prison floor—more than fifty meters.

There was another guard whose job it was to count the prisoners. Each time he would pass my bunk, he'd hit my feet with his clipboard. The guards often took prisoners and humiliated them in front of everyone.

2.

I was conscious about my own actions against discipline. I did not respect their regiment or any of the prison's disciplinary actions or rules.

3.

I didn't stand up when they did head counts.

I wouldn't dress in prisoners' clothes.

I kept my belongings with me, refusing to let the guards touch them.

I never addressed any guard or officer by his rank, no matter how high-ranked he might be.

4.

I was beaten with rubber sticks by guards.

In Pinar del Río, the common prisoners were being instructed by the officials from the state security official to beat me. Later, at Kilo 7 in Camagüey, I experienced similar situations. We all were. It was happening to all of my cohorts throughout the various prisons. Over and over and over.

5.

Braver: From your experiences, why do you think people, such as many of the guards, are willing to hurt other people? Are they willing to torture other people just because they are instructed?

Normando: Look, it is very difficult to get into the minds of these people and consider why they are saying, thinking, and acting so differently than you, especially on what seems like moral terms. But there is a common pattern, at least from a bureaucratic position—the more repressive the officer, the more likely he is to move up the ladder of command.

Braver: And by repressive you mean . . .?

Normando: These officers rejoice after they abuse and torture prisoners. They collect their stories and anecdotes as if they were war trophies. There is only one word to identify them: sadistic.

I once spent months in solitary confinement in appalling conditions without knowing any news about my family, without knowing anything about anyone. Being constantly surrounded by violent criminals two feet away from your bed—both inmates and guards—is constant torture. Sadistic.

Braver: It sounds as if it's about a process of dehumanization.

Normando: Completely. They believe the prisoners are inferior. In their code of ethics, they have positioned the prisoners as their enemies. And with the enemy, as it says in their statutes, no concessions can be made.

Braver: And where do you think their loyalties lie? With the ideologies? The Castros?

Normando: They are people without principles, without ideologies, without convictions. They aren't even loyal to Castro or Communism. If you ask them, many cannot even differentiate between one thing and another—they are semi-illiterates. These are people that come from the mountains and fields of Cuba; that is where they pick-up the things they know.

Braver: So in their minds, it's just a job they're blindly doing?

Normando: Basically, yes. A job where they beat people and torture people. Something they consider better than working in agriculture.

And because they have a license to be guards and wear a uniform, they believe themselves infallible. They'll tell you this outright: "We can kill you and nothing will happen." They told me this infinite number of times, on a daily basis. And the bottom line is that for the most part they are right, nothing does happen.

6.

The dividing line is so thin; it becomes nearly impossible to distinguish between the psychological threats or the physical threats. In the moment, physical torture is painful—it does leave marks on you. But I think that the permanent, constant psychological torture hurts more.

7.

For me, the worst form of torture was in knowing what they were doing to my wife and my little girl.

One time, when I had been isolated in solitary confinement for five months, I finally was awarded some visitation time. My wife, daughter, and uncle made the trip to see me. While my family waited, the guards came up to me, seeing this as an opportunity to win the battle over my continuing refusal to wear the prisoner clothes.

"Normando," one guard said, "if you put your uniform on, then you can take the visit." The other said, "And after your family leaves, you can take it off and can continue doing what you are doing." I said I wouldn't accept their deal.

"So you do not love your daughter? You do not love your wife? They came all the way from Camagüey and you don't even want to go see them over this?"

The other guard shoved the clothes at me. "Put this on!"

I backed away from them, bracing for the worst. "You do not know what principles are," I said. "You don't know what conviction is. And that's what makes you different from me."

The guards turned and left, saying nothing.

Shortly after, they returned with a note that they'd had Yaraí write. It read:

> *We are here: your daughter, your uncle, and I. Our daughter is desperate to see you. She has even been crying. They are not going to allow the visit because you will not put the prison uniform on. But don't worry, I will always be with you. Think, but think wisely.*

The guards reveled in watching me read this. All the while, I tried not to show my suffering.

8.

But, of course, it didn't end there. The next day the director of the prison's services, Dr. Poso, took me up to an office. He was yet another corrupt thief. Poso regularly stole my medication, along with the disposable syringes my wife had sent me.

He said he wanted to talk with me about my daughter; how she was so anxious. He said while Daniela had been waiting the day before, she'd taken out a photo of me—she always traveled with the picture of me—and kept saying, "This is papa, it's papa." And how she'd cried because she wanted to see me. "Listen," Dr. Poso said, "that daughter of yours broke everyone's heart. And all that this silly stance about the uniform proves is that you really don't love your daughter." It was clear how much he enjoyed seeing the hurt this caused. "As you know," Poso continued in false sincerity, "this is an institution of punishment. You know you can't make phone calls. But, if you want, I'll make a call for you. Tell me what I can say to your wife so she can come back. I can negotiate it so that your family can see you."

"Look," I said. "I appreciate you offering to make the call. And there's something very important I'll ask you to convey on my behalf."

He nodded. That I seemed to be buying into this visibly pleased him.

I continued: "I ask that you please tell this to my wife: *Do not worry about me. I may not be living how I would like to, but I have the both of you in my heart*."

He still looked proud of himself, slumped his chair, with his arms crossed over his chest.

"*And lastly*," I finished my recitation, "*do not come to visit me again while I am at Pinar del Río!*"

Dr. Poso gripped the side of his chair. His cheeks flushed. "I cannot tell her that!"

"But didn't you offer to speak on my behalf? If so, then that's what I want you to tell her."

He exhaled, and then muttered, "Yes, of course."

Of course, Dr. Poso never called her. It's how they work. First they build the expectation. Then they follow it with a constant and slow trickle of psychological torture.

9.

State security officials threatened my wife, saying they would tear down our house.

They told my mother they were going to make me disappear. She finally had to leave Cuba. The regular threats against me (and her) wracked her nerves.

Before I was arrested, the state security officials were trying to divide me and Yaraí. If I picked up the phone, they would say she was betraying me with another man. If she picked up the phone, the accusation was made against me.

It was a constant, constant, constant psychological game.

PART FIVE

They Ruined My Health Instead

1.

When I first was incarcerated, I did not suffer from any disease. Other than a chronic allergy I'd always had since childhood, my whole body was completely healthy. But after five months of living in prison, I began to exhibit my first health problems. It started with a lot of stomach acidity. Then I started losing weight quickly, accompanied by bouts of diarrhea. It all left me feeling very weak.

Little by little, this began to increase. The prison doctors said I just had a mild case of gastritis and erythematous in the lower stomach. They said that it wasn't severe, easily curable. But in reality, it was not resolved. My health continued to decline. Those years in prison left my entire digestive system damaged, most notably by a syndrome of bad intestinal absorption, gastroesophageal reflux disease, and chronic colitis.

2.

After some testing, the prison doctors concluded I had polyps in my gallbladder; they said this was a cancerous lesion—carcinogenic—and that I should have my gallbladder gutted. For two years, I was subjected to this pressure; they wanted to cut out my gallbladder but I refused. Periodically, they would give me ultrasounds. Each time, I was told my polyps were growing.

3.

Two to three months before my release, I'd been told that the polyps had grown dramatically, measuring 16 mm and 8mm in diameter. I now ran the risk of these polyps obstructing my vesicular duct, and that if left untreated, eventually I would need an emergency surgery.

My family—my wife, my mother—all told me, "You need to have surgery, you need to have the surgery." But I didn't want it; I knew whose hands I'd be putting myself in. Plus, I never felt any pains in my gallbladder area. "Why are you saying that I have this in my gallbladder if I don't feel anything?" I asked the doctors. "I don't have any problems with my gallbladder." They explained it was a symptomatic problem. The lesions were the symptomatic expressions of something larger.

It was hard to tell what was what. But based on my family's concern, and with no basis for disputing the doctors' claims, I agreed to the surgery.

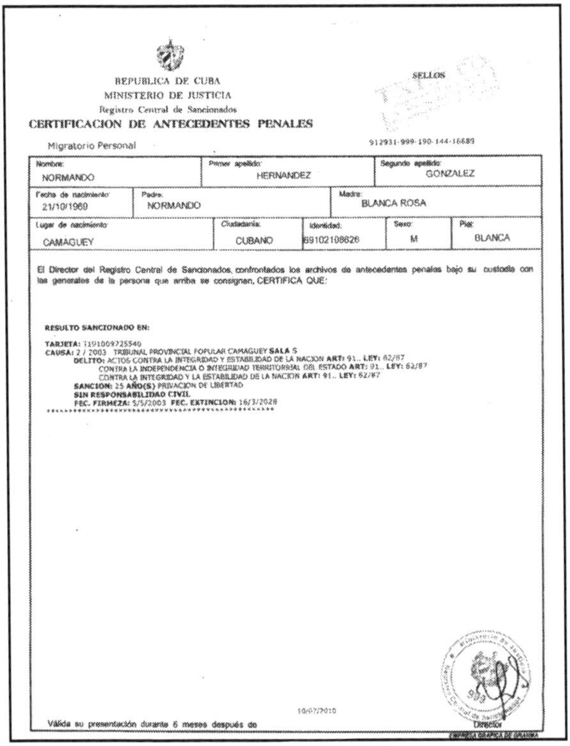

REPUBLICA DE CUBA
MINISTERIO DE JUSTICIA
Registro Central de Sancionados

SELLOS

CERTIFICACION DE ANTECEDENTES PENALES

Migratorio Personal

912931-999-190-144-16689

Nombre:	Primer apellido:	Segundo apellido:
NORMANDO	HERNANDEZ	GONZALEZ

Fecha de nacimiento:	Padre:	Madre:
21/10/1969	NORMANDO	BLANCA ROSA

Lugar de nacimiento:	Ciudadanía:	Identidad:	Sexo:	Piel:
CAMAGUEY	CUBANO	69102108626	M	BLANCA

El Director del Registro Central de Sancionados, confrontados los archivos de antecedentes penales bajo su custodia con las generales de la persona que arriba se consignen, CERTIFICA QUE:

RESULTO SANCIONADO EN:

TARJETA: 1191009725540
CAUSA: 2 / 2003 TRIBUNAL PROVINCIAL POPULAR CAMAGUEY **SALA** 5
DELITO: ACTOS CONTRA LA INTEGRIDAD Y ESTABILIDAD DE LA NACION **ART:** 91.. **LEY:** 62/87
CONTRA LA INDEPENDENCIA O INTEGRIDAD TERRITORRIAL DEL ESTADO **ART:** 91.. **LEY:** 62/87
CONTRA LA INTEGRIDAD Y LA ESTABILIDAD DE LA NACION **ART:** 91.. **LEY:** 62/87
SANCION: 25 **AÑO(S)** PRIVACION DE LIBERTAD
SIN RESPONSABILIDAD CIVIL
FEC. FIRMEZA: 5/5/2003 **FEC. EXTINCION:** 16/3/2028
****

10/07/2010

Válida su presentación durante 6 meses después de

Director

EMPRESA GRAFICA DE GRANMA

4.

In Carlos J. Finlay, a military hospital, surgeons removed my gallbladder.

It turned out there were no polyps. Only small fatty cysts. Insignificant. No different than what most healthy people have.

5.

One of the most prevalent tortures I suffered in prison? The way I was being tortured by the health system. They had been toying with my life since day one. Today I am without a gallbladder, causing me to have many gastrointestinal disorders. You see, the gallbladder emits the bile, which helps facilitate digestion. Without a gallbladder, the bile going directly to the duodenum induces an almost constant diarrhea. I also have gastroesophageal reflux; I practically have to sleep sitting up in my bed.

Ideologically, these people never turned me—they couldn't do what they wanted with me, and they couldn't humiliate me in any way. But they are so low, so dirty, so crass, so cowardly—that they ruined my health instead. It's very difficult to prove that these diseases were the results of being deliberately infected, but the evidence corroborates it. It's not a coincidence that I entered prison as a completely healthy person and that I left the prison a completely sick person.

6.

My health has improved a bit since being exiled. I have gained weight considerably, but I am still not at my normal weight. It's hard to eat anything, the food all settles so badly. It leaves me very weak. I don't have enough energy to feel as strong as I should for my age.

I am very sensitive. Delicate.

PART SIX

They Were Not Able to Destroy Us

1.

We have to keep in mind that not all the prisoners are highly dangerous delinquents. In Cuba, the majority of the prison population are victims of the Cuban government. They are victims of the social system that has been created by the savage communism of the brothers Fidel and Raúl Castro.

And in terms of the guards and officials, there were some I met who were incredibly good people. People who know how to be friends. People with a Christian sense of things, family people. But they were forced to commit crimes to feed their children, to be able to feed their aging parents, to be able to feed themselves, to be able to dress themselves. The miserable salaries the government paid these people were not enough to afford the basic necessities. And that is why these men were forced to commit such atrocities.

2.

In Cuba, even to breathe is illegal. To breathe! If you breathe in the air, and, while taking it in, you don't praise and congratulate the government, you are being unlawful and can be jailed—just for that.

In Cuban penal codes, there exists a crime called *peligrosidad pre delictiva* (pre-criminal dangerousness). *Peligrosidad pre delictiva* means people don't necessarily need to commit a crime in order to be imprisoned. If a court, a judge, or a police officer believes a person *could* commit a crime, then that person can be jailed up to four years. But that's not all, because the law also accounts for so-called "post-criminal dangerousness." Simply put: if after four years the state determines the person originally imprisoned for what he *could* do is not reeducated, then that prisoner can be incarcerated for another four years.

At this point in time, there are about five thousand such inmates inside Cuban prisons.

3.

Many people are prosecuted for the supposed crime of theft and slaughter of livestock. Why? Because in Cuba, the only red meat you can eat is the one the government dispenses in its loan stores, at high prices; nobody can afford it. That means that the farmers who raise livestock are forced to secretly slaughter some for themselves. Sometimes they will take that meat to the elderly; sometimes they'll sell it for just enough to pay for their basic needs.

Just because there is a large quantity of farmers that have been jailed for this supposed crime doesn't make them criminals. No. They are simply victims of the savage communism that exists in Cuba.

But don't get me wrong: just as there are good people like these, there also are very bad people. Murderers, criminals, psychopaths, and maniacs. And, no different than anywhere else in the world, these people are a high threat to society and need to be imprisoned.

4.

It's disgraceful how the Cuban government looks for ways to demoralize us, to discredit us. Thank god—though I have to say it generally like this—they were not able to destroy us; they tried but did not succeed in a campaign of permanent humiliation.

5.

Our work inside the prison was pedagogical, in the sense that we taught prisoners to understand their rights, and how they could reclaim their rights. We educated and explained values and moral virtues and the spirituality of human beings.

And we also did this same work with our repressors—the jailers.

When the state security isolated me from the entire prison population, they were also isolating me from my repressors. They didn't allow the guards to speak to me, much less go near me. It was said that I made them ill, that I brainwashed them. Of course, none of that was true. I simply explained to them that they were human beings with mothers, fathers, and children. And that any one of their family members—or even them—easily could find themselves in our same situation. Would they like it if their loved ones were treated like they were treating us?

We showed them they also had rights; explained that they were the government's slaves. And reminded them that when one is complicit in a crime, then one is a criminal.

I was able to make many guards conscious of the realities we all were living under.

It's like everything, though: there are good people and bad people on both sides.

PART SEVEN

Talk! Talk! Talk! And Never Shut Up!

1.

The state security had full knowledge of the entire effort that my mother was engaged in—both in my defense and in the defense of everyone from my cause. She publicly denounced the Cuban government's authoritanarism. The state security knew before me that she had met with President Bush and Secretary of State Colin Powell. They closely watched her as she campaigned for the cause throughout Europe. The state security had information about everything she did. Where she went. What she said.

2.

It should not be forgotten that my mother, Blanca González, is a political refugee in the United States. She was an activist for human rights before she left Cuba.

The state security made sure I knew that they knew. Standing outside my cell in solitary confinement, they'd report her acitivities. They would tell me, *while your mom continues to scream, you will only see darkness inside here.*

Here's what they didn't get: telling me those things gave me worth and joy. She frustrated the government officials. They couldn't take it out on my mother, so they tried to take it out on me. But I never gave them the reponse they hoped for. Instead, I'd simply say to them, "Before you is a man who will endure all the punishment and torture that you want. But no matter what, my mom is not going to shut her mouth. You can't make her shut up. If you have the desire to take it out on her, then just continue to retaliate against me. Standing before you is a man who is willing to endure anything."

Truly, it was the greatest joy these officials from the state security could ever give me.

3.

My phone conversations with Yaraí were always bugged. Knowing we were being listened to, I'd say, "Tell my mom to remember what I used to say to all the people I met while traveling for the cause. *Talk! Talk! Talk! And never shut up!* She doesn't need to worry about me; I am here to take it and endure. *Talk! Talk! Talk! And never shut up!* I will endure."

That always enraged the state security.

4.

I have to thank my mother, not only in the way all children should thank their mothers for bringing them into the world, but I have to thank her for being my friend and confidant. She is everything to me, and I hope she will be for the rest of my life.

PART EIGHT

Those Moments of Solitude and Total Isolation

1.

There are people who think of family visitations or conjugal visitations as highlights; but in my particular case I cannot say so. I suffered a lot when I knew my wife was going to to travel more than seven-or-eight hundred kilometers to come visit me in prison. I suffered because I knew she was a victim of their threats. And I knew that anything could happen to her during the trip. During the fifteen days before and after her visits (which ocurred every five months), I was always so nervous, wracked with worry.

The actual conjugal visits weren't much better because these people were always engineering a way to humiliate us. Before Yaraí would even see me, they'd try to verbally abuse her, make her undress, or make other degrading requests. And so quite often she already would be upset before she actually arrived. I, of course, was also upset.

We also knew we were being spied on during our conjugal visits. I will never forget the day a prisoner came to me and said, "Hey, last night there were people here who are not from the prison, and they were over by the halls for a long time." The halls are the rooms where we have our conjugal visits. He continued, "They were putting down some cables and other things. I am telling you because I know you'll be going to the halls in the next few days."

"I bet I can tell you which room they were in," I said. "Was it Room 10?"

"Yes. Yes. Room 10! How do you know that if you never are let out of here?!"

"Because Room 10 is what they always give me for my conjugal visit."

His voice quieted even lower. "Normando, you need to be careful not to tell anyone I told you this. It could cost me everything. They'll take away all my privileges. They'll take everything away."

"Don't worry about it," I said. "Don't worry about it."

I went to my conjugal visit knowing that I was being spied on during the most intimate moments with my wife. It was very difficult. I wouldn't want to say anything to her. Who knew what might get her in trouble. On one occasion I wanted to refuse her visit, but Yaraí said no. She convinced me that at least we'd have time to converse, time to speak, and time to be together. This little bit was our only opportunity.

Looking back, those moments that seem as though they should be the comforting ones were the most difficult for me. They represented a perennial unease about what might happen to us, profoundly hurting us deep in our souls.

2.

Knowing you are in an isolation cell being tortured while your wife, your family, and the whole world has no idea about the situation is devastating, if not overwhelming. You have the sensation that no one is listening. That you don't exist anymore. And that no one worries about you. It's as if the sky and the earth are going to come together and crush you. And no one will notice it's happenning.

I'm speaking to you about moments that were very difficult for me, moments that were most trying. Even the moments of physical aggression I faced were never as challenging as those moments of solitude and total isolation.

3.

Seeing the torment of the people next to you was another kind of suffering. I still can picture those sick from leprosy. How their joints became deformed. And because it was dry leprosy, their skin would wrinkle. And they slept on top of the wire beds as the only way to calm the itching. It was all so degrading. Rarely cared for. Left in cells no different than me. They would cry for medicine. Cry for food. Cry to be heard.

I offered them my food. My medications. But they wouldn't accept either. "You are also fucked!" they said. "You are also sick."

"No, no, no. I am fine," I said, lying. "And I have more medication." This also was a lie; most often I didn't have any more.

I felt confident in giving away what I had left because I knew I had a spiritual strength in my soul. But these sick men were alone. They did not have the same capacities. My consciousness always allowed me to endure.

Even today, it still pains me to speak of their suffering. I remember them so intensely, so permanently. But at times I would like to forget. I'd like to forget everything. Everything. Then maybe none of these memories would come into my mind.

PART NINE

They're Going to Set You Free!

1.

I have this tendency to deny my emotions to myself. On the outside, I maintain a calm, distant affect, while the full range of emotions swell on the inside. It's a self-defense mechanism that I developed in times of crisis to keep my adversaries from ever knowing whether I was excited, or afraid, or happy, or sad.

2.

There had been a stabbing in the prison that day, delaying my scheduled telephone call home. Finally, once things got back to normal, I was able to phone.

At the exact moment I reached Yaraí, my uncle was listening to the news on Radio Martí. They were reading a press release from Cardinal Jaime Ortega, the Archbishop of Havana. It said the negotiations by the Catholic Church for prisoner releases had been successful.

My uncle ran into the room, screaming toward the receiver to me, "They're going to set you free! They're going to set you free!"

I asked Yaraí, "What is my uncle yelling?"

"He says that they're going to set you free." And, after putting me on hold to hear what my uncle had to report, Yaraí relayed the information about the press release.

I was still skeptical. I began musing over all the possible angles with her.

Radio Martí then announced they were going to read the press release again. My uncle turned the radio up. I was still talking and conjecturing. "Be quiet!" Yaraí said to me. "I'm going to put it on for you, listen."

And then, through the tinny phone reciever in a prison room, I heard the voice of my friend and fellow journalist, José Luis Ramos, reading the press release.

This is how I found out about what was going to happen.

3.

My wife was jumping up and down. "Maybe by tonight you'll be here at home," she said. "Tonight you'll be home!"

I didn't want her hopes to get too high. "Look Yaraí," I said, measuring my tone. "We need to be patient. Have patience. You heard the Cardinal's statement clearly, right?"

"Yes, and it said that releases should begin in the next few hours."

"Precisely," I said, trying to maintain reason. "The *next few hours* is a very ambiguous phrase. The way these people work, the *next few hours* can be today, or ten years from now."

She breathed slowly. I could almost hear her thinking between each exhalation. Finally, she asked, "But do you believe that? It's a promise to the Catholic Church, the government isn't going to lie to the Catholic Church." This rationalizing wasn't so much my wife's naivety as it was her desire to have me by her side.

"Look Yaraí, this government has been lying for fifty-one years. They lie to the children. To the tens of thousands of political prisoners over the years. To all of us. They lie to themselves."

"But aren't you happy with this news?"

"I am skeptical. I don't believe anything they say. For now, I'm only going to ask two things of you: keep calm and stay strong. And know that if I don't come home tonight, and if I don't come home in the upcoming week, that I will return one day. You don't need to worry."

On our previous visit, I'd confessed that I'd lost all hope of being set free in a short time. I'd explained that given this reality, I'd decided to dedicate myself to intellectual pursuits, in terms of writing and studying (along with everything else I'd been doing for our cause). I was going to strengthen my mind so that they couldn't wound me anymore than they already had in their prisons. In that vistation room, I had told Yaraí that for all the bad we've endured, I believed the worst already had happened. "So please keep calm," I'd said, "because I now feel stronger than ever."

Now, with potentially promising news, I found myself relaying the same admonition. I repeated that despite what we'd heard, it was important to remain calm. "I don't want you to make any mistakes," I told her. "And I don't want you to get desperate or create high expectations for yourself."

Meanwhile, I remained completely skeptical.

4.

Word traveled quickly through the prison. Some of my brothers came up to me. "Hey," they said, "we're going to be set free." As I did with Yaraí, I told them I was being cautious.

They said, "But aren't you happy?"

"No," I answered. "I can't get caught up in ungrounded expectations; it will only be counterproductive for my health." My comrades (and the whole world it seemed) saw me as too serious, too skeptical. But it comes back to those self-defense mechanisms that I developed for survival. I faced things the moment they arose. I didn't worry about what might happen at an undetermined moment. I could only confront life day by day.

There is a saying I once remember hearing: "Either the problem has a solution and it is useless to worry, or the problem doesn't have a solution and then it is useless to worry."

5.

One afternoon, I was brought into the state security office at the prison. Waiting for me was a Lieutenant Colonel, Chief of Military Counterintelligence Department of Safety of the Camagüey province. Although his name is Ernesto, the Lieutenant Colonel insisted on going by a Russian pseudonym, Boris. He was the most evil "person" I'd ever encountered in my life—if I can even use the word "person." He sweated hate out of all his pores. His look was of pure evil. Thinking back, it's incredible that there could ever be a "person" that diabolical.

Ernesto was leaned back in an office chair, with that potbelly of his sticking out at me. "Normando," he said, his tone eneveloped by arrogance. "Take the phone, you have a call."

What was he up to? After more than seven years in prisons, I'd never received a single phone call. Without picking up the phone, I reacted from instinct. I knew what Ernesto was capable of. This was the man who had threatened Yaraí, who had told her on any one of her visits with me that she could easily have an "accident." This was the man who threatened to demolish our house. This was the man who created all the drama at my daughter's school, telling her I was in prison because I had had a bomb and was going to kill all the children. This was the brain—the center—of all evil that occurred around my family, and around all of Camagüey. He was the chief, with maximum power, responsible for everything. "What did you do to my wife?" I yelled. "What happened to my daughter?!! What has happened to my family?!!!"

He leaned forward, holding up his hands, motioning me to stop. "No. No. No," he said. "Your family is fine. The call is not even *from* your family. Go over there and take it. And then we'll talk."

Somehow the lieutenant colonel had become the good spokesman? What was waiting for me?

6.

Cardinal Jaime Ortega was on the other end of the line. "Normando," he began, "in the conversations the church has had with the Cuban government, it has been decided that a group of you will depart for Spain. Initially, it'll be a group of five people; however, you are not in that first bloc of five. You are scheduled to be in the second group of five people. But first, you must tell me, are you even willing to go to Spain?"

"Look," I began, and then caught myself. "First of all, your excellency, I'd like to thank you for all the humanitarian gestures that you've been commandeering. But to your question: if going to Spain means going without with my family, then I'd rather continue as a prisoner."

"No, no, no. Normando, it will be with your whole family. Whomever you would like."

It all caught me by surpise. Yaraí and I had talked about this possibility when some of our brothers of the cause had been sent to Madrid in 2008. She and I had agreed that if something similar ever was offered that we would be willing to immigrate. Still, I didn't quite know what to say.

The Cardinal was patient. "Normando," he suggested, "maybe you should take some time. Think about it. Reflect."

Maybe he was right. There was time. After all, I wasn't scheduled for the first group (I would go—*if* I went—in the second group). But then, without further thought or reflection, I blurted out, "Yes, I will go."

7.

Two things were on my mind: my daughter and my mother. This should not reflect poorly on Yaraí nor diminish her. My wife has always been by my side; a part of every detail. Throughout my ordeal (and before and after), she was my confidant. Our relationship stayed strong. But I hadn't been able to maintain a relationship with my daughter or my mother. I hadn't even seen my mom for years.

8.

I don't remember exactly how many days had passed after my conversation with the cardinal. Maybe four or five? Maybe one? I just have no recollection. All I remember is being in my cell after lunch. I felt so sick, already having vomited up the food. I was praying for the feeling to pass.

A guard appeared. "Normando," he ordered. "Dress appropriately, and then pack up all your belongings. You're going to be transported." *Appropriately*. I may not have been in the prisoner's clothes, but I was wearing pajamas, which seemed perfectly fine.

As lousy as I felt, I still replied, "I am always dressed appropriately."

There is always a battle with them.

9.

I already had everything more or less put away. I always lived that way, a factor of always being transported from here and transported to there.

They led me to a patrol car that came from the state security. We were going to Ciego de Avila, where we would pick up the other brothers from our cause who were in this second round bound for Spain. From there, we would be driven to Havana.

10.

As soon as they put me in the vehicle, I thought I'd pass out. And we weren't even moving. The man in charge of the operation asked what was wrong.

I told him that due to my health I didn't think my body could bear to be transported. Remember, it had only been a month since the gallbladder surgery. I was still in very delicate health. In fact, the last time I'd been transported to the hospital in Havana, they had to give me oxygen. Otherwise I'd have fainted, overwhelmed by the nausea.

The man said, "No, no, no. Come with me." That's how I came to find myself traveling with the head of the operation in a car with air conditioning, one of those new Chinese cars that were being brought to Cuba.

11.

They only gave Yaraí half an hour! Half an hour to abandon our house, to abandon our home. My wife, my uncle, and my daughter. Simply half an hour. In half an hour, she had to decide what she was taking with her. And in half an hour she had to leave behind her entire life. Her entire life.

My daughter is incredible. Daniela gathered her toys and movies, and she went to her friends' houses and gave them all away. She is exceptional. She gave them all of her toys and her clothes. And for those friends who were not there, she left packages for them with neighbors, dividing everything up evenly. Everything she left in Cuba, she left to everyone, to all the people she loved and cared for.

12.

In Havana, we were brought to the national hospital for prisoners in Combinado del Este prison. They placed us in an air conditioned room, one that typically was closed to prisoners. For the few days that we were there, they gave us a quality of food we'd never had while in Cuban prisons. It was amazing, like hotel food, prepared with incredible care. This is where you can see how evil these government people are: they actually have decent food to give to prisoners, but it never gets to them. But, still, we weren't fooled. The intention of the excellent treatment was obvious: over the five or ten days while we waited, they hoped to brainwash us into forgetting the hunger and the torture and everything else we'd been subjected to over the course of seven years.

13.

Gessford: During those few days at the prison hospital, while waiting to leave Cuba, and being well taken care of, did you feel any sense of relief?

Normando: I really didn't feel any sense of comfort—quite the opposite. I knew they were up to something, but I couldn't clearly identify what it was. I was only guessing by the way they acted. Now, after being exiled, and trying to make sense of my guesswork, I realize that I was not wrong.

Gessford: Meaning?

Normando: They were only trying to improve my physical appearance so that my frail condition would not cause too much of an impression when I arrived in Madrid. Also, as I mentioned, it was something of a concerted effort to make me forget everything that I had just suffered for so many years.

Gessford: Was there ever a moment when you feared you might be vulnerable to this strategy?

Normando: The contempt felt by the Cuban government representatives for those who oppose them is something that is actually good for us. It helps us to remember their point of view: that we are inferior and therefore unable to think and act correctly. Being vigilant about their baseness keeps us from falling continuously into their traps. So, no, the fear of being persuaded by my enemies never crossed my mind.

14.

On July 14th, along with my fellow brother in the cause, Omar Rodríguez Saludes, we landed in Madrid. It was just Omar's family and mine in the airplane. They dressed me and Omar in long sleeve shirts, trousers, and ties. The only things I had were my luggage and a suitcase full of books—(of course no novels, stories, or literature that even suggested anything political, as those had been banned in the prisons). The few things I had from my cell had been given away to prisoners who needed them a lot more than me.

Clothes and books. They were the only things I arrived with.

15.

I feared my daughter's reaction, and well—she had an incredible reaction. We have a picture that I think is historic because it was right when we first saw each other at the airport just moments before boarding the plane in Havana.

My daughter started to run, and didn't stop until she was hugging me. And I hugged her back. Then Yaraí came to us, and all we embraced. Someone said, "Hey! Look over here . . ." The three of us turned to see a photographer snapping a picture of us. My daughter held up her fingers in the sign of victory—a peace sign.

PART TEN

Another Field of Combat: Exile

1.

Imagine a tree, one that has been uprooted and planted in distant lands. In autumn, it begins to take root, and by spring its branches leaf and flower. Eventually, the tree will grow so big it will bring shade and coolness to the land which bore its first fruits. I work to become a nest in that tree, where all the longings and sufferings sit side-by-side with the joys of life; a nest set on a branch that covers my land, and then extends across the sea to the land of my birth. One nest among many branches, among many such trees, solid in their strength and in their hearts.

The fight for freedom and democracy in Cuba—before, during, and after my experiences—needs these types of trees that are capable of withstanding the onslaught of tryants who are dedicated to cutting them down, hoping to keep oxygen from the people.

2.

Leaving prison was like being born with experience. This experience goes a long way when I find myself far from all I know, when I face new challenges and cultural patterns, and when I'm confronted by political, economic, and social conditions that are so different than what I'd been indoctrinated to over my lifetime. After having suffered so much, and for so long, nothing scares me. I face life with renewed vigor, excited to regain the lost time. Everything I do is motivated by love.

3.

Bittersweet feelings enveloped me when we first arrived in Madrid. It was overwhelming and exhausting. There was no question that I was happy to be beside my daughter in a free country. I'd only lived with Daniela for her first twelve months, and now, already, she was eight. Also, it was pure pleaure to wake each morning beside my wife, and to be able to talk freely with my mother, who now was living in Florida. But at times, these wonderful feelings could vanish when I thought of all that I'd left behind: work as a freelance journalist in the frontline battle against the government; family, and friends from childhood, youth and adulthood; and the memory of my brothers still in prison, living under the filth created a totalitarian regime for fifty-two years. Night and day, it continued to hammer away at my brain.

There was no question that I needed to continue the fight.

Every day, I told myself, "The fight does not end. It continues from another field of combat: *exile*. Never surrender under the grip of the hands of those who enslave you."

4.

Physically, I'm in Spain, but my spirit and my life is in Cuba.

5.

The Spanish government, insisting that my being exiled was having traumatic effects on me, suggested relocating me from Madrid to Cullera, a city in Valencia, hundreds of kilometers away from the capital. I believe their motive was to disseminate us dissidents throughout the country, so that, effictively, we could not continue our work of bringing attention to the Castro brothers' totalinarian regime. Of course, I didn't want to go. Being away from the city would make my work for freedom and democracy in Cuba that much more difficult.

You see, the Spanish government's Ministry of Foreign Affairs and Cooperation, led by Miguel Angel Moratinos, had been waging a campaign within the European Union to remove the Common Position that had been imposed on the Cuban government in 1996. By disguising our banishment as a release, the ministry believed they could present a strong argument to the European governments to withdraw the Common Position, predicated on the idea that Cuba's human rights record had improved. This certainly was motivated by Spain's economic interests in Cuba. Moratinos seemed dedicated to trying to clean up the image of the Castro brothers' regime. That is a major reason for why he worked to refuse us political asylum status—if we were granted that status, this would only confirm to the international community that the totalitarian regime still prevailed in Cuba. And, of course, that was why the Spanish government did not want us to leave Spain to particiapate in international forums—by allowing us to honestly depict the true realities of life in Cuba, we also would be exposing the bad foreign policy of Spain in this regard.

6.

One day, Mr. Agustín Santos, Director of the Cabinet of the Minister of Foreign Affairs and Cooperation, arrived at the Welcome hostel where we'd intially been put to live with our families. In a forceful and threatening manner, Mr. Santos tried to demand that we leave Madrid for the various regions they had suggested. Again, we refused. As a last resort, Mr. Santos tried to spread feelings of guilt among us for our decision not to leave Madrid, telling us that we would be responsible for keeping our remaining brothers in arms imprisoned in Cuba.

Pressure came from all sides. Members of the Spanish Red Cross treated us with contempt. Many of us we were very sick when we'd first arrived. But our complaints fell on deaf ears. The Spanish Catholic Commission for Refugee Aid (CEAR is its acronym in Spanish), was not far behind, with its clear apathy for us. They did not expect that we would protest; they planned on hearing very little from us once we arrived in Madrid. I always suspected that there was tremendous corruption within those organizations, and that they were profiting from the resources that had been allocated to us. It seemed they were clearly colluding with the Spanish government to make our lives difficult life Spain, taking direct orders from the ministry.

In general, it seemed as though Spain was looking for ways to make us feel as if we were still prisoners, wanting to control our lives. Sometimes it didn't feel much different than daily life in Cuba.

But thanks to supportive friends and the Cuban community in Madrid, we were provided with all kinds of advice and help that allowed us to withstand the pressures of the Spanish government and to be able to stay and reside in the capital of Spain. The president of the Community of Madrid, Esperanza Aguirre, was particualarly integral in finally being able to get us specialized medical care, as we still were recovering from the effects of years of torture.

And soon enough, many of my friends and relatives began to appear (many crossing the Atlantic from the U.S.), giving us all kinds of help—from baby food (which was still all I could digest after what the prison did to my digestive system), to clothes, shoes, and money. (It should be said that these visitors also brought many supplies for my brothers and their families who also had been banished.) This outpouring of generosity helped ease our coming into exile, with one foot in Spain, while the other was still left behind in Cuba. Because of the support of friends—from abroad and within Madrid—my family and I did not feel like aliens in this new world.

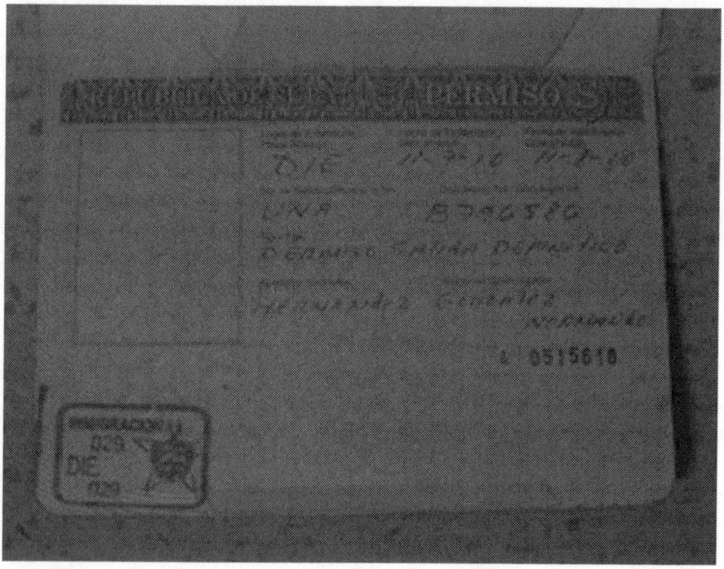

7.

For ten months, I've lived without a defined legal status. Having come directly from prison into exile vis-à-vis the agreements between the Cuban Catholic Church and the governments of Cuba and Spain, and based on the international recognition that Amnesty International accords prisoners of conscience from the moment of an unjust incarceration, we should have been granted political asylum status the moment we arrived here. But we were not.

Armando Valladares, former Ambassador to the Human Rights Commission United Nations during the Reagan administration, told me that he had reliable information that part of the agreement between the governments of Cuba and Spain for our release was that we would not be granted political asylum. The Cuban government understood that if Spain were to grant us political asylum, it would be tantamount to an international recognition of the largest existing tyrannical regime in the Antilles.

It seems that Mr. Valladares was right, because the pressure for us not to ask for political asylum status was tremendous. Agustín Santos became obsessed with trying to have us granted with a status that he called *International Protection.* Santos argued that if we requested political asylum status that we would never be able to return to Cuba. We just looked at him dumbfounded. He seemed to forget that our passports were stamped *Final Exit*, which, under rules imposed by the Castro brothers, meant that we could not return to the land of our birth.

Many of us brothers-in-arms were confused why Mr. Santos still would not ask for political asylum status. And we felt blackmailed. For example, when we were invited to other countries to testify about our experience in Cuban prisons, the Spanish government declared we could only travel if we gave up our applications for political asylum. Although I always applied to go, I was never allowed. I wouldn't submit to their terms. I refused to be blackmailed.

Again, we received support and advice from the Spanish solidarity members and the Cuban residents in the capital of this great nation, and they assisted us in hiring lawyers to demand our rights. Now, ten months later, we are finally in the process of having our rightful status granted.

In my case, I may not get it in time, as my family and I hope to be in the United States permamently, reunited with my mother, who is now a U.S. citizen.

8.

Even banished from my home country, I found ways to further my work. I was connected with the Spanish People's Party and other European politicians who were committed to defending the freedom of the Cuban people. Along with two brothers of the cause, I was able to take my case to the European Parliament in Brussels. We went to various parliamentary committees, sharing our experiences as prisoners of conscience in Cuba. In the committess, and in individual meetings, we urged the MEPs to continue the EU's Common Position, to maintain the policy that guides the EU's relations with Cuba, based on encouraging democracy, respect for basic freedoms and human rights, and an improvement in living standards. You see, the position was subject to review and updating every six months; it was important for keeping the Cuban government on notice. We also lobbied the MEPs to grant the Sakharov Prize for Freedom of Thought to our compatriot Guillermo Fariñas, a great crusader in the cause for a free Cuba. Not long after we left, we learned that the European Union continued the Common Position, and Guillermo Fariñas was awarded the Sakharov Prize 2010[5].

In Poland, at the invitation of the Lech Walesa Institute Foundation, I participated in a conference on whether a free Cuba was a dream or a reality from the perspective of Europe.

But, as mentioned earlier, due to the blackmail by the Spanish government, I had to miss a conference in Germany with the International Society for Human Rights (of which I am honorary member and partner), held on December 10, the anniversary of the Universal Declaration of Human Rights.

In March 2011, I also was gagged by having my travel to Norway refused. I had been scheduled to give a lecture to Spanish students at

5 On December 14, 2010, the BBC reported that "the Cuban authorities have refused an exit visa for a leading Cuban dissident to travel to France to receive the EU's Sakharov Prize for Freedom of Thought . . . Instead the Cuban dissident will be represented by an empty chair."

the University of Oslo and then to meet with prominent Norwegian politicians and intellectuals.

On March 18, 2011, along with four brothers, I met with Mr. Christian Leffler, the EU's Managing Director of the Americas (he reports to Catherine Ashton, the High Representative for Foreign Affairs and Security Policy, who is charged with finding approaches for a closer relationship between the European Union and Cuba). We handed him a ninety-six page report that made the case that any change that has occurred in Cuba after our exile has only been to go from bad to worse. In order to better shape the EU's future reports and policies, the report also encouraged a delegation of the High Representative to travel to Cuba and meet with the real civil society to learn more about what life was actually like on the island.

Meanwhile, when I could, I continued to visit the embassies of different European countries, presenting them with the report we delivered to Mr. Leffler. I was able to let them know that we'd been reassured by Mr. Leffler that Catherine Ashton had confirmed that any EU approach to the Cuban government needed to be within the framework of the Common Position, and that she'd agreed that a delegation would travel to Cuba and meet with the true civil society.

Over these past ten months my work in Europe for the freedom of my people has been intense. Media interviews. Conferences. Government meetings. Speeches. But it's the least I can do. I won't rest until I see Cuba free of the Castros' despotism.

9.

Just last night, I had a dream, a nightmare; it woke my wife up. I told her that in the dream I was fighting with the guards and with the prisoners whose beliefs I found most offensive. And the only thing I could think to say in the dream was, "Out with Fidel! Out with Fidel! Out with Fidel! Out with Fidel! Out with communism! Out with communism!" That was it. In my nightmare I'd lost my voice. I could not speak.

Inside the prison, I never had these nightmares. Now, I have them regularly. They are the remnants that remain. I would like to forget, but, unfortunately, I cannot forget.

10.

My daughter Daniela just turned nine. She wants to forget. She rejects everything that has to do with Cuba—any commentary about the island, photographs or videos, and journalists that want to interview her. Daniela entirely rejects everything because these things trigger her memories—they lacerate her. In Cuba, because of the trauma of my situation, she received psychiatric and psychological treatment. But as much as she wants to forget about Cuba, inside her there is a self that will not allow her to forget. Proof of this is in the poetry she writes. It is all related to the evils of the Cuban government—essentially, her denunication. At only nine years old, instintively knowing that the past may be stronger than her, Daniela uses poetry to express herself; it's the way she can speak out.

The last poem she wrote two days ago, said, "We all know how hard it is to be human/ but we don't all know how hard it is to be Cuban/ and to live in the clutches of a tyrannical government." She can express the effects of complex political situations because she has lived it in her own flesh since the day she was born. And this is how it is. Everything is very difficult. But we have to overcome it because there are people who have suffered much more than we have. And we are a living testament.

11.

Unfortunately, I cannot forget, because forgetting all of that human suffering would mean forgetting a part of my life. Forgetting all of this human suffering would make it so I could not adequately help the people who, in these very moments, are suffering what I have suffered, if not much more. Forgetting all of this human suffering would mean not revealing this to the whole world, so that the wills of the global citizenry could unite and take some measure against what is happening in Cuba—primarily with the prisoners.

That is why I want to forget, but I cannot.

It is something that is very difficult for me at times like these.

United States Senate
WASHINGTON, DC 20510

May 21, 2010

Raul Castro Ruz
President, the Republic of Cuba
c/o Cuban Mission to the United Nations
315 Lexington Ave.
New York, NY 10016

Your Excellency:

Based on shared values of human rights and humanity, we respectfully urge you to release prisoner Normando Hernández Gonzalez and the 25 other political prisoners who have been identified to have serious illnesses. As you know, Mr. Gonzalez was arrested in March of 2003, along with 74 other journalists considered to be dissidents by the Cuban Government. He was sentenced to 25 years in prison for violating the terms of Article 91 of the Cuban Criminal Code.

We understand that on February 25, 2009, Mr. Gonzalez was discharged from a Havana prison hospital and sent back to Kilo 7 Prison in Camagüey. He is reported to have contracted Malabsorption Syndrome, which has led to malnutrition, heart disease and anemia, all of which are exacerbated by his incarceration. He is also suffering from a growth on his Adam's apple. While reports indicate that the prison doctor has visited him, this is no substitute for the medical attention he so urgently requires. As of November and December of 2009, accounts have suggested that Mr. Gonzalez's health continues to fail at an even more alarming rate, with complications in his heart, gallbladder, and gastrointestinal system. The state of his health remains our utmost concern.

While we may have political differences and diverse perspectives, a respect for humanity is one area upon which we can agree. Sharing this common ground, we urge you to release Normando Hernández Gonzalez, and other political prisoners with serious illnesses, on humanitarian grounds and to urgently allow them to receive proper medical care.

Thank you for your attention.

Sincerely,

Jack Reed
United States Senator

Sheldon Whitehouse
United States Senator

Editors' Note

While all of the words in *Normando Hernández González* come from the interviews conducted in March 2011 in Madrid, we have taken editorial liberties in terms of structure and chronology—all for the intended purpose of clarity and narrative structure. It was all done with the consent of Normando.

It is also important to note the support of the Spiegel Center for Global & International Studies, and the Department of English & Creative Writing at Roger Williams University; Larry Siems, Anna Kushner, and Sarah Hoffman at PEN American Center; photographer and educator, Jeffrey Silverthorne; students at Roger Willliams University who, in many different ways, as part of school's collaboration with PEN, worked and advocated for Normando's release while he was still imprisoned; Bill Lavender; the good people of UNO Press; Cynthia Guardado, not only for her translating, but for not running for the hills when she realized how much there was to do; Oscar Peréz, the onsite translator and guide in Spain; Michael B. Gessord, for his wisdom and inspiration; Normando's mother and tireless advocate, Blanca; and lastly, of course, Normando, Yaraí, and Daniela for welcoming us into their home, lives, nightmares, and hopes while in Madrid.

—A.B. & M.G.

Biographies

Normando Hernández González was born on October 21, 1969 in Camagüey, Cuba. As an independent journalist, he was part of the group of seventy-five dissidents who were arrested and tried 2003 in what is now known as the Black Spring. Hernández was sentenced to twenty-five years in prison. Following a series of negotiations, he was released and exiled to Spain in 2010.

Among his awards and distinctions are the *PEN Barbara Goldsmith Freedom to Write Award*; the *Dr. Rainer Hildebrandt International Human Rights Award*; the F*undación Hispano Cubana International Human Rights Prize*; and the *Cuba Corps la Orden La Demajagüa*.

Hernández currently resides with his wife and daughter in Miami, Florida. He continues to work as a practicing journalist, as well as serving as Director General of the Cuban Institute for Freedom of Speech and Press, a nonprofit NGO created by him to defend the inalienable freedoms of the Cuban people.

Editors

Adam Braver is the author of five novels. His books have been selected for the Barnes and Noble Discover New Writers program, Borders' Original Voices series, the IndieNext list, and twice for the Book Sense list, as well as having been translated into Italian, Japanese, Turkish, and French. He is on faculty and writer-in-residence at Roger Williams University in Bristol, RI.

Molly Gessford lives in Boston, where she teaches English as a foreign language. While earning her BA at Roger Williams University, she interned for the PEN American Center. Her writing has appeared in the *Providence Journal*, the *Bristol Phoenix*, and the *Normal School.*

Translator

Cynthia Guardado is a Salvadorian-American poet and currently attends CSU Fresno's MFA in Creative Writing. She has previously been published in *The Acentos Review*, *The Packinghouse Review*, and *PALABRA*.